DEDICATION

THIS BOOK IS DEDICATED

WITH LOVE

TO THOSE WHO MADE IT A REALITY.

ISLAND OF KNOWLEDGE

ISLAND of KNOWLEDGE

BY LINDA QUIRING

CCB Publishing
British Columbia, Canada

Island of Knowledge

Library and Archives Canada Cataloguing in Publication
Quiring, Linda, 1944-, author
Island of knowledge / by Linda Quiring. -- Second edition.
Issued in print and electronic formats.
ISBN 978-1-77143-198-9 (pbk.).--ISBN 978-1-77143-199-6 (pdf)
Additional cataloguing data available from Library and Archives Canada

First edition published by the Sydney Banks Spiritual Foundation, with layout and design by Golden Temple Printers.

Except for the addition of the Author's Note*, this second edition is a reprint of the original first edition from 1975.

Publisher: CCB Publishing
              British Columbia, Canada
              www.ccbpublishing.com

* Publisher's Note: The only other changes made were corrections to blatant errors that appeared in the first edition from 1975, as follows: 1) Roman numerals for Chapter 19 in Table of Contents and chapter heading corrected, 2) Title of Preface corrected from "Forward," 3) Chapter 5 title in Table of Contents corrected spelling of word "Fictitious," 4) Page 39: spelling of word "salal" corrected, 5) Page 56: spelling of word "its" corrected.

AUTHOR'S NOTE

Before friend, confidant and teacher Syd Banks passed on in 2009, we discussed reprinting *Island of Knowledge*, the book we had written together in the early 1970's.

We both agreed that the counter-culture jargon I'd used at the time, such as "trippy," "far-out" and "games" were outdated, and frankly, a little embarrassing. We discussed whether it would be better for an edited version to be put out.

More recently, discussing the book with Jack Pransky, who helped bring this project to fruition, and Paul Rabinovitch, my publisher, we wondered how to re-present the book. Would it be best to edit the work, refresh the dialogue and get rid of the hippy-type pictures of the day?

As we contemplated these changes, it became clear that editing the book would be complicated. What exactly should be left in, what should be changed and what taken out?

The book is a personal account of what took place on Salt Spring Island, British Columbia in 1974. The words in the book are Syd's own, before psychologists came to the island, and well before he began using such terms as "The Three Principles" in his spoken and written words. Syd's enlightenment experience had occurred only a year before, thus in a sense it is an important historical account.

Furthermore, the photos, beards and 'highs' quite accurately depict an amazing time and place when dozens of young spiritual seekers sought out an enlightened man, Sydney Banks, whose teachings are still changing lives and inspiring students over forty years later.

What happened in *Island of Knowledge* was the beginning, the spark that ignited everything that followed. I decided that to tamper with the integrity of the book would be a great disservice, thus it is printed exactly as is.

Linda Quiring
Salt Spring Island, May 2015

PREFACE

This is the story of how I moved to a small island to find myself, and the amazing encounter I had with an unknown prophet named Sydney Banks, someone who very few people even knew existed.

His teachings are so powerful and so full of love that it is impossible to hear him and ignore his wisdom. He changes the lives of all whom he touches.

His explanation of how Self-Realization is obtained has the validity of pure truth and the results are breathtakingly beautiful. He is indeed a miracle-worker on Salt Spring Island.

December, 1974
Linda Quiring

CHAPTER I

I MEET A PROPHET

Salt Spring Island is a tiny island just off of the Pacific Coast near Vancouver, British Columbia. After leaving the ferry you see mountains, valleys, lakes, huge arbutus trees, shaded dirt roads and peaceful little farms. There is a small village with a harbour, fishing boats, a post office, a fire hall and a few stores.

The first thing I noticed were the people. They were so casual, so friendly, and everyone always seemed to have all the time in the world. The whole atmosphere of the island was so unbelievable that after the first day, we'd decided to stay. Neither Bill nor I had a job or knew anyone on the island and I wondered what had brought us here. But we'd both been searching for something and had the feeling that good things would happen.

Then we met Sydney Banks and felt he was the reason for our being here. We heard he was giving groups on higher awareness and decided to see what he was all about. After going to several different types of groups and not finding what we were searching for, we were interested in a new group, but pretty cynical.

Bill and I went over to have coffee with Syd and his wife, Barb. They live with her mother Mary and their two children Susie and David in a far-out old house on the ocean with forest all around. On one side of the living room is a fireplace and on the other side are windows which look out on the water and some other small islands off in the distance. At night huge freighters come by lit up like Christmas trees and a while after a boat has gone the waves start hitting the shore in front of the house. They come roaring in and become louder and louder until suddenly it is quiet again and the fire is snapping and crackling and the vibes in the room get higher and higher until it's the most peaceful place in the world.

I talked to Barb first and although living out in the country and doing a real family trip, she was very aware, very wise and gentle. Sydney is an incredibly beautiful person, of medium build, dark, blonde hair, a little on the long side, and a beard and mustache. I had the impression of his being very agile. He's extremely loose, flexible and extraordinarily relaxed. When you look into his eyes and talk to him you feel the charisma. Peace and love radiate from him.

We sat around talking about the island and our children and every once in a while Syd would say something about the Self or about playing games, and it became more and more interesting. I had the feeling that SYD KNEW. I tried to ignore it but as he talked my suspicion became stronger. It blew my mind. You just don't move to a little island, go down the road and meet some fellow who knows!

Now I wanted to find out what and how he knew. I'd read many books on awareness to find the answer and it hadn't worked, and I asked Syd what he'd read. His reply was, "very little, perhaps four books."

"But you see", he continued, "The answer is not in books. It cannot be written and it cannot be spoken. It must be experienced. This is what our group, if you want to call it that, will be about. We will neither be interested with the past nor with the future but just the here and now.

"We must forget what life has taught us and keep clear and open minds. We must not be misled by past experiences and thoughts. If we think and try to rationalize, all we are doing is stopping our growth.

"We are taught we must think to find a solution. In higher consciousness we find that things work the opposite way. After all, it is our thoughts and hang-ups that got us into this mess in the first place."

Now Syd was saying that I must stop thinking to find higher awareness. I just didn't understand. I'd been busy thinking for years about how to find happiness and then someone tells me it's not going to work. Throughout the conversation I became more and more excited. Maybe this way was different, but it might be the right way. Syd appeared extremely happy and peaceful all the time. I asked him about the group and what the trip was.

With a smile, he answered,

"We are searching for true Self, the source of everything on earth. There are two ways of finding the secrets of the universe. One is by following the religious path to realize God. The other way is to realize true Self by finding out who you really are and what you really are, and what all of your games in life are which keep you in this illusionary state of believing that what you see is real. Now whether you find true Self or God, it doesn't matter. They are both the same. I prefer finding Self, but that's my trip."

Wow, this was really heavy. Here's a fellow thinking about everything being an illusion and he's sitting right in front of me. I didn't know if he was crazy or for real.

I said, "Surely that table is real."

"Of course it is real to you, at least that is what you think. It is only because of what you have seen and heard

3

and all of your past experiences from life that make you think that the table is real. You are controlled by thoughts from the past and the present. You will have to learn to drop those thoughts if you want to see life clearly."

Bill then told Syd that he had been at many awareness groups and some of them did him a lot of good, but not really enough to keep him happy.

"I keep searching and searching in one group after another. Now I am getting fed up with the whole trip!"

"Obviously you are not really fed up with your trip, as you call it. You are here today. This proves that you are still searching. Let me put it this way. When you first started on your journey towards finding yourself, the group you joined at that time was perfect for you. Your level of consciousness has obviously grown since that first group. Now that you want to go deeper into finding yourself, of course you feel confused! The groups you have told me about sound like World War II has started all over again.

"You say they pushed each other, shouted at each other, and verbally and physically fought. They condemn each others actions, then usually end up pretending to themselves that no matter what anyone did in the group it was O.K. and everyone forgave everyone else. If everyone is so forgiving where did the hostility in the group come from? I am absolutely sure if you really looked at this question the answer would be "yourself". Now imagine if everyone in the group "truly looked" each individual would come up with the same answer, that is, 'I am to blame for the hostility!' Now if everyone truly saw this, there would be no hostility, only love and understanding.

"This is a very difficult thing to see, because very few people know what their deeper games are! They are usually completely non-existent to the individual. It is not until

4

you experience the knowing of these games that you begin your journey into higher levels of awareness. In my opinion anyone who runs awareness groups full of negativity is too superficial. They don't truly believe in the Self, nor do they understand the meaning of violence.

"You are an example. You have arrived at a stalemate. You feel unsatisfied. You are searching for something new, yet you don't know what you are searching for. In actual fact you haven't any true power or knowledge, only the superficial knowledge you have picked up from outside influences. On one level this is true yet on another it is false, because you really do know what you are searching for! Someday you may find these words to be true and when you do, it will be a lovely experience.

"One should never rush the process of learning. Just be there when the knowledge appears. Be 'Here and Now'. Then you will know you are in the right place at the right time, no matter where you are. Just be now! There is no end to knowledge, believe me, no end! Yet it is the most beautiful and fruitful journey of your life. It is so devastatingly mysterious and yet so simple, it is absolutely fascinating!"

"Syd, are you saying that you are against workshops unless there is a person in a high level leading it?"

"No, I am not saying that. You see, a workshop is as high as the highest being in the room. Now, if this is so, everyone else in the room has the opportunity to learn. How can the workshop be considered negative if there is an opportunity to learn?

"Once a person arrives at the stage where his enquiry is deeper than the group is capable of handling, then the group is of no value to that person.

"On the conscious level of thought it appears we all

5

have free, individual minds. This is 'true'. However, on the sub-conscious level we are individualized but think and act according to the law of God. This law of God is well hidden and cannot be explained. Everyone on earth must act according to the unknown law! When one realizes Self, one realizes this hidden law and is free from all bondage. Here we have another dual answer. Although one is free, one still has to comply with this law of life.

"When one realizes this law is governed by love and understanding, one serves Self willingly, knowing there is nothing wrong and everything is exactly the way it should be."

"Syd, why do you try and change people's lives if everything is 'as it should be'?"

"Let us say you are a mixed-up person searching desperately for Truth. That's exactly what you should be! On the other hand, if you hear words of wisdom which change you and you become a much more content and wiser person, then that's exactly where you should be."

"You have begun to know truths, therefore you are on your way to planning your own destiny. This is the beautiful thing about the Law of Self.

THERE ARE NO BONDS HOLDING YOU PRISONER

EXCEPT FOR THOSE YOU IMPOSE

UPON YOURSELF

BY THOUGHT.

YOU ARE A FREE MAN

BUT DON'T KNOW THIS TO BE TRUE.

* * * * * * * *

The word 'game' was continually coming up in our conversations and I questioned Syd about it.

"What exactly do you mean when you tell us we are all playing games on each other? I really don't like the idea that I play games on myself and others. I imagine the word 'game' as always being negative."

Syd thought for a moment, then looked at me and said, "Life is an illusion but we play it as real. This is the game of life. Therefore everything we see or do is part of the game. It is the law of nature.

"The idea of the game is to find your Self. This is made very difficult because we encounter much negativity in life, that is, hostility towards others created by competition, envy, greed, desire, and so on. These feelings stop us from seeing what is true and from being happy and content. As you begin to know your inner Self more, the less negativity you will have in your life.

"I think it is very important to start looking at EVERY-THING you do or anyone else does as just part of the game. Someday you may start to enjoy seeing all the games that take place when people meet. If you can see your own games, then you will see others playing their games and this is a most enjoyable state. In this state you do not judge people negatively, you just KNOW they are 'playing their game'.

"They are as they are and have no other choice. They aren't aware of their acts nor do they know they are acting. So how can they be blamed for their actions?"

Bill and I were certainly receiving a lot of 'food for thought' and Syd told us to come down any time and we would continue our talks.

CHAPTER II

THOUGHT -- A DANGEROUS ENEMY

One warm fall day in September we were again at Syd and Barb's to continue our search into awareness. Bill turned to Syd and said,

"Sometimes I'm amazed when I look around and see the terrible mess the world is in."

"But everything is exactly the way it should be at this moment."

Syd's answer shocked Bill.

"I don't understand you saying 'everything is as it should be.' What about the starving people all over the world, the wars and the unjust distribution of wealth?"

"I am not saying things could not be better, nor am I saying that if people looked at the inhumane situations around them they should not change them for the good of humanity. What I am saying is that we control our own destiny. This is what our folly has created, therefore it is exactly as it should be. You see, life is a game, just a big game. We have complete control but don't know this to be true. Because we are unaware of the fact that we are the controller, we no longer have control, only folly. There are very few people on earth who have the slightest inkling of what life is all about. We live our lives thinking what we see is real, but we don't see it at all. We are blind. If one 'SEES', one 'SEES' the folly behind it all. Then he can use controlled folly.

"'Life is a figment of our own imaginations.' Now if

this is so, you could say it is like having a dream. When you dream, you feel pain, love, hate, and believe they are real... It is real! True Self is playing games with you. If you learn to control your dreams you will find out that you have the same control awake! It is your choice whether you want to feel sad, happy, disappointed and so on. You create your anger to suit yourself and the particular game you want to play at the time of choice."

Bill and I were somewhat confused, and we looked at each other in disbelief over Syd's words. Bill told him that what he had just said didn't seem to make sense.

"Perhaps if you were hearing me instead of listening to yourself you would hear something."

"But I'm listening to you and I would be more than happy if I could hear and understand you."

"I know you are trying hard. Perhaps this is your problem. Maybe you are trying too hard! Don't worry Bill, as you start to experience the knowing of your Self you will become braver, then what I say to you will start to make sense. You aren't alone, everyone must face this fictitious fear on their journey to Self-Realization.

"You see, most people are so blind they cannot see beyond their conditioning. They see only what they want to see. Oh yes, they pretend to themselves and others that they are open-minded and unafraid of any new experiences, but there are very few who have the courage to look at the Truth. It is futile to even imagine that awareness can be taught. It is strictly up to each one of us to face his own fear. Facing this fear is the true teacher.

"In other words, you are both teacher and pupil. If you know someone who 'knows', you are very fortunate. His words of knowledge and what he tells you, you already know somewhere. It is then up to you to decide whether or not you are brave enough to look at yourself and face the Truth."

Barb said,

"I find it hard to believe that everyone knows the Truth."

"If you don't know the truth about yourself, who does? I've told you before many times and once again I say, 'We are totally all the same.' There is no difference between you and me or any other person on earth. We are all the same and somewhere we know this to be fact. If ever you do find out that this is so, you will be amazed at the simplicity of it all. You will start to love people for what they are, not for what they are not.

"In talking about awareness, you will be humble and patient with others because you will know they are facing fear which consciously they don't even know exists. Also you will never play any power games on them because there is no need to. Instead of negative power games, you will feel humble, knowing you are one with the other person.

"Sometimes it is necessary to play games and shock people, but only for their benefit because once again they must face fear. It is like saying, 'If you can't reach them through the front door, try the back'. Both doors lead INSIDE and that's where the truth is.

"Have you ever known anyone who got a high from a workshop or T-group who didn't first go very low? Probably they cried or felt awful about themselves. In reality all they have done is faced a fact about themselves then temporarily accepted it and by this acceptance they felt really great or 'high'. The only problem is that usually they keep on thinking about it, fear creeps in and they are back where they started. This is why

THOUGHT IS A DANGEROUS ENEMY.

ONE SHOULD NOT

THINK OR ANALYZE ONESELF!

"Accept the fact that what you are doing now or what you did in the past is right for you. If you try 'not thinking' you will soon realize in higher awareness that things are opposite. If you think about awareness you will get nowhere. If you do not think you will obtain beautiful results!"

"Syd, why do you say we are all alike when everyone has their own distinct personality?"

"The trouble here is not letting go of the body! I realize we all look differently and act differently but INSIDE we are all true Self playing the same game, the 'Game of Life.' We all play the 'ego' and everything that goes with it. We all play insecurity games, such as 'poor me', 'dig me'. We have jealousy, envy, hate, desire, and anger. All these feelings that I have just mentioned have to be fed to keep them alive.

"You must learn how to destroy those negative feelings and leave only positive ones, then you will be full of love for yourself and others.

THIS DESTRUCTION OF

THE 'BIG EGO'

IS DONE BY

THE 'NO THOUGHT' PROCESS.

That is, simply not thinking negative thoughts which the past has taught you. The idea is for you to ACCEPT the inner games you play, then they will have to vanish."

As Syd talked about thinking negatively, how it makes us feel, and about talking negatively, I began to realize how I could bring myself down by thinking about something. I was always doing this because I would think about Bill and maybe I shouldn't have become involved, or I would worry about getting sick or depressed. But Syd kept talking about negative thoughts and soon I began to be very aware of them. Soon I would think, 'Hey, I'm thinking about this and it's going to make me feel bad.' But after a couple of weeks I'd think, 'This is a negative thought, I'll think about something nicer!' And it worked. I'd bring in some positive thoughts and I'd be up again.

CHAPTER III

DISCOVERING GAMES

One of the first things Syd told us was that 'we create our feelings.' Furthermore, we are those feelings. We create the feeling of sadness or anger, or whatever. My first reaction to this was 'what nonsense. I'm mad because Bill did this or that and I don't have anything to do with it. *He* made me mad.' Then I began to notice that if the same thing reoccurred when I was really high, I would ignore it and there would be no anger. So I was creating the feelings after all. If I wanted to get mad I'd just find a situation or a topic I knew would create friction and maybe start arguing with Bill or someone else, and sure enough, sooner or later they would fall into the trap, play the game and say something I could use to create a negative feeling.

I noticed that Bill did the same thing. We were using each other to make ourselves feel low. Once we knew what we were doing, we started occasionally catching on. We'd start arguing about something and then both realize what we were doing and stop, and things would be cool. Or I'd catch him doing it and I wouldn't play my role, so there'd be no hostility. Or he'd find me doing it and tell me and it would be all over. We became closer than we'd ever been and became more open and trusting and more honest about what we were feeling.

Syd was still telling us about life, the game of life,

and I began to notice that other people played their little games too. Everybody played the game in different ways, but we were all playing it. I gradually started to pick up on other people doing the same thing, playing their game, and instead of getting angry at something I didn't like, I'd just think, 'They're into their game, and its O.K., everything is just as it should be.'

We talked it over the next time we were gathered at Syd's.

Carol said,

"I've found many of my games, but I can't drop them. To me it's almost impossible to drop them."

Syd replied,

"You have only discovered the superficial games that you play. There are games connected to outside influences and low level conscious states. We must get into your INNER THEATRE and tap games which are so deep that you don't even consciously know they exist, at least you pretend you don't know. If you ever SEE one of these games, and accept it, you will fly as high as a kite. It will be a most beautiful and fascinating experience.

"With this acceptance, not just knowing the game exists but truly accepting it, the games will start to vanish by using the 'no thought' process. You don't have to try, it will just happen. 'No thought' cannot be explained, only experienced. I hope you will be brave enough to experience what I mean, then you will be on your journey into higher awareness."

Occasionally I became very irritated at Syd, I'd say something and then realize what I'd said, really realize it, and I'd look over at Syd and he'd be laughing, like he knew it all the time.

Once in a while I fall into paranoia. Like, hey, he's got all this power. He knows, without knowing anything about my past, everything about me - what I'm afraid of, when I'm high, what my games are. I asked Syd why the past was so unimportant.

"One must forget the past," he replied.

"It is dead as if it never had been. Start looking at yourself NOW. I am going to be me, not what someone else wants me to be, that is, the past. We hang on to the past because somewhere we know it and feel safe with it. Any new experience regarding me, I, It, or whatever, is a threat to our ego, so we remain cowards, yet call ourselves heroes.

IF MAN COULD ONLY SEE

EVERYTHING OPPOSITE

REGARDING HIMSELF,

HE WOULD KNOW

HE IS SEEING THE TRUTH.

"When one becomes fully enlightened, reaches Satori, or whatever you want to call it, at that moment he is totally dead.

IF ONE LEARNS TO LIVE,

TOTALLY DEAD

THE UNIVERSE IS HIS

AND EVERY SECOND OF

HIS LIFE WILL BE JOY."

* * * * * * * *

We sit around sometimes in front of our fire, or theirs and talk. Syd talks about the total game, the master plan, and we become extremely high, and perhaps get a small glimpse of something, a flash of the universe, a scheme of things. Or maybe feel, Wow, everybody in this room, we are all the same, the same person? The same thing? The same energy? The same consciousness? But the second you begin to think about it - bang! It's gone. I just had it and it's gone. Yet this microscopic second of time changes your life. You haven't got it yet, but now you know it's there.

I feel that Syd has something very precious and almost unattainable. Perhaps it's total love. He has it and if I want it, I can have it also.

At times I become so extremely high and happy, it's hard to believe! I know it's not the ultimate happiness, but it's so much better than what was before. Every now and then I'll think 'What's going on here?' and then I'll think, "I've been having a great time for three weeks. I haven't gotten angry or upset. What's happening?' I feel great, so I really lay a trip on myself and it's down to some serious business. Somewhere I feel guilty about being so happy and I do some washing and cleaning and get quite up-tight. And Bill and our son, Gary better smarten up, don't they know life's supposed to be serious. You can't just go around being happy and having a good time forever.' Sometimes that's all there is to it and sometimes I really get into it for a few days. But I know what I've done and it's only temporary and soon I feel great again.

CHAPTER IV

YOU ARE YOUR OWN GURU

When we went to Syd and Barb's, even if we had just dropped in for coffee, we usually began talking about awareness. Somehow one of us would always bring up the subject and Syd would be there, waiting with a smile on his face and his explanation or answer. These times were very casual and pleasant and we felt we invariably came away feeling better and much higher. On one of these occasions Syd was working on his fireplace, changing the white brick to rock which they had found on the beach. It was beautiful to see him working, just as happy and relaxed as always. He began without a plan and just fit the rocks in and let it happen. The rocks were cleaned and came out all different colors - browns, blues, greens and oranges. Mary said he should be proud of creating something so lovely and he replied,

"I am sitting looking at a beautiful fireplace which is part of my illusion. My labor was a labor of love, therefore when I look at it, I see a fireplace which has sprung up from nowhere and joined my illusion."

Bill and I agreed that the more often we listened to Syd, the higher we became. Most of it was too high to comprehend but we were absorbing a lot. Our relationship was definitely changing. We were noticing some of the games we played on each other and although we still

played most of them, now we sometimes knew we were playing them. A good part of Syd's words seemed to go in one ear and out the other, but every once in a while something would happen and we'd remember him saying that we were hearing more than we knew.

I said to Syd,

"At one time I thought you had no particular method or trip but now I see it as being so subtle I can't figure it out. It's like the power of suggestion. Every time you say something will happen, it happens and it's beautiful."

Syd explained,

"But you see, it's not me that makes it happen, it's you! I don't make anything happen to you. No one has the power to make you do anything against your will. When I talk to you about the secrets of life, it is only those who are ready that hear. I merely show the way! You are the one who has been brave enough to look inside and find the answer, the answer you have known all along."

CHAPTER V

FACING FICTITIOUS FEAR

Syd had mentioned that everyone on their journey to Self-Realization must face their own fictitious fear and it was happening to Bill and I now. We began to notice the fear manifesting itself in various ways. When Bill didn't want to hear he would usually fall asleep or become ill.

One night he became violently sick to his stomach, as he had done for years in difficult situations, only this time he realized there was nothing physically wrong. It finally became very apparent to him that he had become afraid, and being sick was a way of receiving sympathy and attention.

"I knew I was making myself sick. I just knew it, but I still couldn't make myself stop doing it."

A game he had played for years was out in the open at last and he had discovered it by himself.

My fear was a little less conspicuous, but there nevertheless. Being afraid is one of my favorite games and in almost any situation I can call upon it. In this way I can disregard what is actually happening in the present and in this way I become unaware of Syd's words. When this happens, I do not hear what Syd is saying. I am thinking,

"Why is he doing this for us? What is he gaining? He doesn't make any money at it and I'm sure that if we never returned he wouldn't become upset or angry -- why does he do it?"

It was happening again, Syd was talking, people were asking him questions, and I was afraid. I was very cold, perspiring and my heart was beating rapidly. All at once I knew why I wasn't hearing him! How could I hear? I had manufactured a lot of negative thoughts and these were tearing through my mind in a rapid stream drowning out anything Syd might say. Knowing I had the power to create the whole feeling, I destroyed it. I began to purposely feed in positive thoughts and shortly after I was hearing Syd and feeling fine. I'd had a brief experience of 'I am the creator, I am the destroyer.'

Bill still played his game at times and so did I, but knowing we were creating the games and knowing that somewhere we were in control made it less real. When it happened, I'd just think, 'Well, here I am doing it again' and the feeling of fear would fade away.

* * * * * * * *

Carol asked Syd,

"If I meet someone who knows, how will I know for sure he is a truly enlightened person?"

Syd replied,

"Don't worry about it, the Divine Powers have their way of guiding.

"If you are ready and you meet a knowledgeable person, you will know. On the other hand if you meet a knowledgeable person and you are not ready, you will only see another body just like yours. This will lead to competition with your new-found friend. You won't see him as he really is, only the way your negative thoughts see him! You with your big ego will be the loser. This simply means you are not ready and if you are not ready there is nothing you can do about it."

"That must make lots of people hostile towards you when they can't understand?"

"Of course, the lower the conscious state the person is in the less they hear, therefore the more hostility appears to defend the 'ego'. On the other hand, the ones who do hear love and respect me. Those who can't really make up their minds about me fear my words, yet remain because they are interested. There is an old Tao saying:

> *"The great rulers -- the people do not notice their*
> *existence*
> *The lesser ones -- they attach to and praise them?*
> *The still lesser ones -- they fear them?*
> *The still lesser ones -- they despise them.*
> *For where faith is lacking, it cannot be met by*
> *faith.*
> *Now how much importance must be attributed*
> *to words!"*

"These are not just words. It is a fact. People according to their level of consciousness MUST react in this manner."

CHAPTER VI

LOVE IS THE SECRET

We soon met again as friends, to visit and have a good time. On this particular day, Barb came to the door. We hadn't seen her for two or three days and the change was unbelievable! She was absolutely radiant. Her face seemed to glow and she looked years younger and full of energy. We knew something had happened and Syd remarked she had entered into a higher level of consciousness. Barb had seemed very happy before, but this change was unreal!

We joked about her having a new face cream or beauty secret and she replied, "Yeah, Second Debut." I laughed and I felt we were all happier and more joyous because of her and for her.

Dave said,

"I know it's got something to do with sex," and Syd and Barb just killed themselves laughing. Barb replied,

"I've had an experience of knowing that 'I am the feeling of sex. I am sex."

"Love" said Syd, "is something that can neither be bought nor sold. It is something which must be experienced. The feeling of true love is a beautiful UNDERSTANDING state. It is a feeling of tranquility, a peace beyond normal logic. True sex comes into the same category. True sex, like love, is also a state which denies logic, yet surpasses logic beyond the wildest imagination because true sex knows there is no outside world to dictate logic from. It is supreme honesty

INSIDE and the results are super-supreme beauty and love.

"Sexual freedom is also related to this state! One must realize

SEXUAL FREEDOM

IS FOUND

ONLY INSIDE ONE'S-SELF

Any regard to objects other than Self will reduce sexual freedom.

TO BECOME SEXUALLY FREE

ONE MUST NOT JUST HAVE SEX,

ONE MUST BE SEX.

IN TRUE SEX

THERE ARE NO HIDDEN GAMES

WHICH TURN SEX INTO

SOMETHING IT IS NOT.

I felt this was something I really didn't understand and was relieved when Syd asked David to read something he had written about how he sees himself; how he sees life. As Dave started to read it was obvious he was in a beautiful high space, full of love and happiness. He began and his words were clear and to the point.

"If you are ever to begin your search into yourself for the Truth, you must first begin to doubt your present idea of what is real and what is make-believe. You must begin to experience new psychic spaces which are totally different from what you have experienced before and which have a validity to them that is so powerful and so RIGHT as to make you begin to suspect your normal states and ways of being. If you are to experience something new you must first be open and available to these new experiences. To be open and available you must not be busy thinking of past experiences but be contented to the extent that you can leave past experiences and be more in the present moment. You must be happy and contented and accepting of the present moment as O.K."

As he read Dave's voice began to break. He was overcome with emotion and his eyes filled with tears. He could no longer continue reading his own words and said he was crying because of the love he felt for himself and for everyone else. Turning to Syd, he said,

"The secret is love, isn't it?"

Syd smiled and replied,

"Yes, it's beautiful."

A silence followed as we all felt the love and beauty of Dave's words and his obvious space. He said,

"Wow, it's sure powerful stuff when you enter into these higher planes."

Once again the room was full of energy and a great warmth spread among us as we each felt, as far as we were able, the place of joy that Dave had tapped into.

On the way home, I felt happy for Dave and Barb, but soon began to drift into thoughts of "Why isn't it me?" The old ego again. "Why can't *I* feel like that?" I began to feel worse and worse and spent the next couple of hours feeling sorry for myself, envying their space, being angry at Bill and trying to bring him down.

Finally Bill said:

"Let's just pretend we're happy. We'll just try it for a couple of hours and see what happens, O.K.? If we don't like it we can always go back to feeling sad."

His face was so earnest I had to laugh in spite of myself and soon gave up trying to be bummed out. We had some tea and a fire, and watched an old John Wayne movie, made love and spent the next days feeling great and having a ball.

CHAPTER VII

SELF-IMPORTANCE
Vs.
PERSONAL POWER

Feelings of guilt were beginning to drift into my consciousness and the next time we gathered together I mentioned this to Syd.

"I sometimes feel guilty because I am doing this trip, searching into myself, and I am becoming less interested and less involved in other things. I feel I am shirking my duties as a member of society."

Bill said he felt the same way.

"If everyone had a lackadaisical attitude like us who would be responsible for getting things done? What about helping those less fortunate than ourselves?"

Syd looked at us both and replied,

"The trouble is with you two is that you think too much. You're so damned hung up with your own self-importance you won't look at anything new."

When Syd said this I became angry immediately and told him how I felt,

"Syd, I really resent you saying I am full of self-importance."

He began to reply but all at once I realized what a contradiction my words were. I was denying that I felt self-important yet had begun my denial with an "I". My resentment seemed utterly ridiculous then, and everyone laughed along with me at my discovery.

Syd continued,

"You must start to realize that you are not the world, just a grain of sand in the middle of the Sahara Desert.

"Now this does not mean you should shirk your responsibilities as a person in this Karmic world. What I really mean is you will know you cannot change the way things are. 'They are as they are because they ARE.' This is the way of God-Self or the energy of All. It is you and you alone who picks your own path and your own destiny. Once you start collecting power then you will go faster on your journey to knowledge of Self.

"The knowledge you seek is NOT out there in politics nor is it found by wealth or power, nor is it in fighting for the liberation of others! Liberate yourself first, then you can afford to help others!"

"I am sure" said Barb, "that if we really looked at the question just asked, the question isn't really who is going to help those less fortunate, the question is why are there any less fortunate at all? Surely it must be because we as people are so selfish and greedy we simply don't want to look at ourselves and find the Truth."

Syd replied,

"You see, my friends, there will always be takers and givers. There will also always be people in between helping others which is a very beautiful thing to do. Lastly, there are those apprentices searching for Self. These apprentices cannot afford to get caught up in life's busy stream lest they be swept away by the undercurrent of ignorance. It is only when one truly starts to see oneself that he finds peace and love and understanding."

Carol then asked Syd if he could give his definition of 'self-importance' to help us understand.

"Self-importance is thinking you are important in this life. You must realize that in Reality we are nothing but pure energy playing the game of life with the illusion of the body'. One must get away from the body into Self-consciousness! At this point one will realize that we are all the same, hence I am no better or no less than you. We are all equal INSIDE. We are all the same source playing the game of life, our game of life is identical. Yet in our known life as humans, it is ridiculous to think we are all alike! No two people are alike, we all have our outside differences."

"By outside differences do you mean our own physical characteristics and personalities?"

"Yes, that is correct. Our physical and personal characteristics are all different on the body-mind level. When you go beyond mind THEN we are all the same.

"Somewhere everyone knows this to be true. If you ever find Self you will see it is no great thing to understand. As a matter of fact it's a very simple thing to understand. The only thing that stops you from SEEING this, is your thoughts of 'what is and what should be' or 'what is false and what is real.'"

"Syd, earlier you mentioned us 'starting to collect power'. What do you mean by this", asked Mary.

"Personal power is what we are searching for. Personal power cannot be given to you, although you can virtually pick it up from anybody or anything you wish! The problem is that most people don't know what personal power is. They have never EXPERIENCED the possessing of it, therefore they don't know what it is!"

"But, Syd, you've taken a lot for granted saying most people have never experienced the possessing of it. How do you know what other people have experienced?"

"If you really knew what personal power meant, you wouldn't have asked such a question. Believe me, as you begin to experience power it becomes greater and greater, then you begin to see things differently. You will also act differently. You will act the way you want to, not the way you were taught to act.

"Your personal power will protect you from seeing things incorrectly. This personal power always guides to positive actions. Just the fact that you are here on earth makes it your birthright to find this wonderful power and spend the rest of your life in a happy world, instead of a frightening, chaotic one.

"Sometimes absorbing personal power can be a bitter battle and one has to pay heavily for gains, but after the battle is over it is ALWAYS worth it! Now most people don't have a clue who or what they really are. They know their name and their profession, which are outside influences. Personal power is what takes you from outside influence to inside influence. If you ever get brave enough and challenge death you will know the Self outside and the Self inside. You will have become one with both outside and inside. When this happens everything looks beautiful."

"I still don't understand!"

"Personal power cannot really be explained, it must be experienced."

Syd looked as if he were searching for words, then looked up and said,

ONE COULD SAY

PERSONAL POWER IS

THE AMOUNT OF PERSONAL KNOWLEDGE

ONE HAS OF ONESELF.

THE MORE YOU BEGIN

TO TRULY KNOW YOURSELF,

THE MORE CONTROL

YOU HAVE OVER YOUR LIFE.

THEREFORE THE OUTSIDE INFLUENCES

HAVE LESS CONTROL OVER YOU.

CHAPTER VIII

REALITY Vs. ILLUSION

One afternoon in November we went to Syd and Barb's and found the family down on the beach in front of their home. The day was very warm and pleasant with just a hint of the cold to come. They had built a huge fire out of driftwood and we all sat around the flames, with the ocean and gulls in front of us. We were talking about love and the source of all life. Syd was working away with the fire when he turned around and said,

"To accept love we must have love within ourselves.
The more love we have within, the more love will
        flow
And life will become more and more beautiful.
If we are tormented inside and void of all love,
        it is impossible to see or feel love,
no matter how many people offer it to us. We
        must
first love ourselves before we can love at all!"

"Everyone originally stems from the "I", "The True Self", "God" "soul", or whatever you wish to call it.

"This source is pure energy. As you appear to yourself you are a figment of your own imagination. This source creates all of your senses, love, hate, jealousy, sadness. Totally everything is controlled from this source and if you ever truly realize this, then you, as you know yourself will become the controller. At this realization you will know there is no separation between you and the true energy source. We are as one! You will realize also that there is no separation between you and anyone else or any other thing on earth, for we are all the same energy.

"This is what we call the game of life. Your body is nothing but solidified energy and when you die the true you is still the same as ever. Just the body ceases to exist. That is, until you choose another! The difficulty in realizing this is the fact that we must face total fear and be willing to give up our body and life as we now see it. When we do this, we find out that we haven't given up anything at all. We also realize we have always known this fact. How beautiful to know we are fear, we are love, we are hate, we are everything which creates us."

Mary said,

"Wow, that's heavy! Did I hear you say that we pick our own body?"

Syd replied,

"Sure, why not?"

We all laughed and then silence followed as we realized we were all totally confused. He told us not to worry about it, that everything comes to those who are brave enough to look.

* * * * * * * *

I had never been out on the ocean in a small boat before, so Bill and I took the canoe out for a ride. The water was calm with hardly a ripple and so clear we could see the crabs and oysters among the seaweed and rocks on the sandy bottom. We paddled along looking at the shoreline, seeing other houses nestled in the trees and sections of beautiful beach covered with logs that had drifted in. Everything was so quiet and calm and we felt very close and were enveloped in the peacefulness and solitude of the scene. Bill said he wished he could sing, he would like to sing to me because it was our first canoe ride, and the whole day had been so lovely.

We returned to the fire and everyone was still talking awareness.

Barb said to Syd,

"I have read many times that there is a guardian protecting the secrets of life which can take many shapes and forms. Is this true?"

Syd replied,

"Yes, although everyone sees the guardian differently. Everyone creates their own guardian. The guardian in reality is nothing but thoughts.

THESE THOUGHTS

STOP YOU FROM SEEING!"

I told Syd I honestly couldn't see how thoughts created what he called a guardian to stop us from seeing.

"Do you mean to say if I stopped creating thoughts, I would SEE?"

"Certainly! That's what I have been telling you all along!"

At this point we all looked dumbfounded and Syd burst out in fits of laughter and said,

"There you go again, you're thinking and analyzing!"

We all sat around the fire until after dark. The night was becoming cool but it was warm near the fire and I stared at the flames until I seemed to go into a trance. Everything was so peaceful and so quiet I felt I could just stay there forever, listening to the waves. We finally went up to the house and had some oyster chowder that Mary had made. It was so delicious and hot, and so good to have after being out in the cold. After we ate, we were all overcome with drowsiness and Gary, our son, Bill and I went home with lovely warm feelings of having had another perfect day with good friends.

CHAPTER IX

THE JOYS OF LEARNING

It was the middle of November and the winter rains had just begun on Salt Spring Island. The trees that had been dry and covered with dust became clean and green-looking. Our house was nestled in the middle of the forest and huge cedar trees drooped right down unto the windows. Clumps of ferns and salal grew everywhere and rain glistened on the leaves. Winter would soon be settling in and I was in a great space. Bill had been vaguely upset for a couple of weeks and one day left the house for a few hours.

He later told me what had happened.

"I went over to Syd's feeling down. You and I were not as close as we had been in the previous weeks. Some of the trust was gone and I felt scared because I didn't know what was happening. I asked Syd for his advice and he said, 'Bill it's jealousy. You're not aware of what you are doing. You are not in control and what you see is real to you so you are not to blame. You are jealous of Linda writing a book and afraid of her changing and you want to stop her growth.'

"At first I felt defensive and then I saw it. I was afraid and trying to stop you from growing and in that way was stopping myself. It was a negative game and it made me feel negative. After admitting what I had been doing I became high at once and

felt love for you and wanted to phone and talk to you."

When I saw Bill after this incident he was smiling and said he was feeling really great. He went right up after his discovery and stayed high for weeks and weeks.

During the time that followed, I noticed that as he went up, I went down. It vaguely occurred to me that I might be on the same trip as Bill had just been on. I suddenly thought of phoning Syd and asking him for advice, but with the thought came the instant realization that it was true. Wow, I was jealous of Bill and afraid that he would become higher than myself. I was competing with him and went down and tried to take him with me. But I was the loser because I was into a negative game and it was taking the joy out of my life.

Instantly the realization put me into an incredibly great space. It seemed as though with every new piece of knowledge about myself a heavy burden slipped from my shoulders, and I felt this relief every time I discovered a game. The rewards of listening to Syd and believing in him were beyond my wildest dreams. When these 'highs' appeared it seemed that life had never been so good. I loved Bill and Gary and everyone else and the feeling of love was so overpowering that every day was so beautiful. All thoughts of past and future would disappear and I would be in the moment to moment joy of being HERE and NOW.

I told Syd what was happening in my life and he gave me these words:

"ONCE A PERSON KNOWS

THE GAME OF LIFE

AND KNOWS ALL HIS OWN GAMES

HE KNOWS EVERYONE'S GAMES

BECAUSE

WE ARE ALL THE SAME SOURCE.

WE ARE ONE

WITH NO SEPARATION

EXCEPT FOR

THE ILLUSION WE HAVE OF OUR BODIES.

ONE WHO KNOWS OTHERS IS WISE

ONE WHO KNOWS HIMSELF IS ENLIGHTENED.

ENLIGHTENMENT AND WISDOM

CANNOT BE SEPARATED

THEY ARE TRULY ONE!"

Island of Knowledge

CHAPTER X

GIFTS FROM A PROPHET

We were visiting one evening and Bill was expressing the delight and affection he felt for Barb's mother Mary. She was a very far-out lady. Mary spends a lot of time looking after the garden and you often catch a glimpse of her going by with a wheelbarrow full of something in the yard. Her hair is snowy white and her eyes are so young and alive. It is hard to believe she is in her seventies.

Bill said to Barb and Syd, "She just sparkles. Was she always so young and beautiful?"

They told us she had changed a great deal since she began listening to Syd's words.

A few days before she had been sitting in the living room thinking and then walked into the kitchen and said to Syd,

"You know, Syd, I used to feel that the only way I could be happy was if you were gone, and now I feel because of you I am in the most enjoyable, fascinating time of my whole life."

* * * * * * * *

We were on the subject of dreams and Syd told us we could obtain a lot of power from our dreams if we knew how to go about it.

Judy, a girl who had come to listen to Syd's talks, told us of a recurring dream.

"I dream I am flying. Sometimes I have the power to fly as high and as far as I wish. Other times I can only fly a few feet off the ground. Suddenly I become aware that I am in control. I realize it is MY dream. If I want to fly, I merely do it instead of pretending I can't. Then I can fly, really fly!"

Syd grinned and said,

"This was a marvelous thing to have happened. Being aware of a dream is a way to collect more power fast. You are lucky inasmuch as you have established a way to re-mind yourself it was a dream. It takes practice, but you will be well rewarded for your courage."

"Is there any end to knowledge, Syd?"

"No, there is no end. Even people who reach extreme levels of knowledge are learning every day.

IT IS A BEAUTIFUL JOURNEY

FULL OF NEW EXPERIENCES

LEADING TO MORE AND MORE

KNOWLEDGE OF SELF!

THE MORE YOU BEGIN TO ACCEPT YOURSELF,

THE HAPPIER YOU BECOME.

THE HAPPIER YOU BECOME,

THE MORE YOU WANT TO

GET DEEPER INTO SELF.

IT IS A JOURNEY OF LOVE

BECAUSE EVENTUALLY

IT LEADS TO

PURE LOVE.

When we were home later, Bill was really flying high and he began talking about his new, joyful experiences. His face was so calm and beautiful and his gestures and words so alive that it was impossible not to be high along with him. He said,

"Wow, we're so damn lucky to know Syd! Imagine knowing such a wise man, a prophet, and we can just go over and talk to him anytime. I feel so close to Syd and Barb, they're doing such a great thing for us and it's so much fun. The last few months have been the happiest of my life. I'm not interested in making money or travelling anymore. I'm devoting my life and my energy to finding my Self. It is the best thing, the only thing I can do for myself, for you, and for everyone else."

A GIFT FROM SYD

DESIRELESSNESS IS LOVE

DESIRELESSNESS IS HAPPINESS

DESIRELESSNESS IS BEAUTY

DESIRELESSNESS IS CONTENTMENT

DESIRELESSNESS IS BEING NOW!

OH WHY? OH WHY?

DO I DESIRE SO MUCH?

WHAT STOPS ME FROM PIERCING

THE HEART OF DESIRE

SO THAT I MAY BE ALL

THOSE BEAUTIFUL FEELINGS

THAT I ONCE WAS?

CHAPTER XI

"SEEING" IS FREEDOM

Barb and Syd had invited us to visit friends with them in Nanaimo. We took an early morning ferry, then shopped and had lunch. When we arrived at the friend's home the conversation immediately turned to awareness.

Obviously very interested in Syd's words, they had talked with him previously. He was asked,

"You have told us about 'Seeing'. What is the difference between seeing as we do and the SEEING you talk about?"

Syd thought for a moment and then replied,

"TRUE SEEING CANNOT BE EXPLAINED

IT MUST BE EXPERIENCED

'SEEING' IS TRULY SEEING THE TRUTH

WITHOUT YOUR THOUGHTS

DISGUISING WHAT YOU SEE

AS AN ILLUSION!

"These thoughts stop you from seeing 'what is' instead of 'what isn't'. Believe with all your heart what you see is an illusion. The pure Self is responsible for all the illusions that you see. Become one with the illusion, then you will find that which you have always known. 'It is your illusion'. Once you have faced this illusion you will find Reality! You will be well rewarded!"

When Syd talked 'illusion', I was lost. His friend was also puzzled and said,

"Syd, when you talk about illusion I don't understand. What about something more practical to me right now? I'm worried about my relationship with my parents. I love them yet sometimes I can't stand being around them."

"Surely you must see it's impossible to love a person and not want to be around them! What you feel is not love, it is a deep-seated child-parent so-called love relationship. It's a natural way to feel, we are conditioned to believe we MUST love our parents. When we don't we feel full of guilt. This guilt is coming from you.

"You have to try and ignore your conditioning. Get inside yourself and find those negative thoughts which separate you from others.

"This is fighting for freedom. The trouble is we blame our parents for their actions towards us and how they try and hold us prisoner. In actual fact it is we who hold ourselves prisoner. Freedom is not outside away from your parents. Freedom is INSIDE. If you find freedom, you will realize your parents are doing what they have to do and are unaware of their actions. As long as you keep playing negative games towards them you will make them feel badly and you will suffer. Try and truly forgive them, after all they are only conditioned as you are. Try and understand them, put yourself in their place with an understanding that the conditioning we receive from society is a difficult thing to overcome. If you ever do find your freedom, you will love your parents!"

CHAPTER XII

SELF-REALIZATION -- "KNOWING"

Friday had come again and we met as usual. Dave and Carol and their four children, Jo-Ann, Coleen, Pamela and Donald lived on Mayne Island nearby. It was an hour or so by ferry and so they came over and stayed on Salt Spring every weekend, to visit and to continue their search into higher awareness. We were all getting to know each other better and to really trust one another. The whole atmosphere of the group was rapidly changing in a beautiful positive way.

Carol asked Syd,

"How long do you think it should take to realize Self?"

Syd scratched his head and then looked up and said,

"As long as you want! You can realize Self right now if you wish!"

"But Syd," Mary wondered, "I thought our karmas had to be paid in full, we had to be pure before this supreme state could be reached."

"THESE ARE YOUR THOUGHTS STOPPING YOU FROM

BELIEVING YOU ARE GOD.

THE TRUE YOU IS THE BODY, THE EGO, THE KARMA,

THE BIRTH AND DEATH OF YOU.

IT IS TOTALLY ALL OF YOU

INCLUDING THE WORLD YOU SEE.

"If you ever SEE this is so, you will know karma was just part of the game of life, which stemmed from your ego. There is no karma and never was. It only exists in your mind, put there by thought to keep the game of ego going."

David asked,

"Once you know, can you forget you KNOW and what is knowing?"

"Knowing", Syd went on, "is knowing there is really nothing to know, so how can you possibly forget you know?"

"That's impossible!" said Barb. "There must be something to know!"

"Knowing truth is not a FACT as you would describe a fact, because source has not created fact. The truth or knowing is beyond creation. If is Self-God. Knowing is absolutely unexplainable! Even the 'thought' of the word EXPLANATION proves you haven't understood the word 'knowing'."

"Wow, that's sure a mouthful," Barb said, then burst out laughing.

"I take it from that there won't be any further questions?" said Syd.

Everyone in the room burst into laughter and someone shouted,

"Put that in the book, it's good for a laugh!"

Once again everyone laughed and the feeling in the room was high and overwhelming.

CHAPTER XIII

WE DISCOVER 'NO-THOUGHT'

Dave and Carol had come over from Mayne Island and we were gathered together, talking about 'no thought'.

Carol said no thought fascinated her even though she didn't understand it. She thought she had experienced it but could not relate her experience in words.

"All I know is my positive highs are becoming longer and longer. Is there anything I can do to create more of these beautiful experiences?"

Syd replied,

"An exercise which I think is invaluable is to simply sit in a quiet room, close your eyes and think only positive thoughts. This is a good way to sharpen your mind to practice 'no thought.'"

"I feel it is impossible to think positively without any thoughts," said Carol.

"I realize you will be mind-thinking while doing this exercise, but 'no thought' has nothing to do with 'mind-thought.

'NO THOUGHT'

IS THE JAMMING OF NEGATIVE THOUGHTS

BEFORE THEY REACH THE CONSCIOUS LEVEL

IF YOU HAVEN'T ENOUGH POWER

TO STOP THESE NEGATIVE THOUGHTS

YOUR LIFE IS

COMPLETELY OUT OF CONTROL."

"How can we possibly learn to do this?"
"You can't, one has to experience it."
"Well, then, how can we experience it?"
Syd replied,

"GET TO KNOW YOURSELF

YOU WILL GET

MORE AND MORE INTO YOURSELF.

YOU WILL BEGIN

TO EXPERIENCE THE FEELING OF LOVE

THIS FEELING OF LOVE AND 'NO THOUGHT'

ARE COUPLED TOGETHER LIKE LOVERS.

AS YOU BECOME

MORE ADEPT THIS LOVE WILL GROW

UNTIL SOMEDAY

YOU MAY REALIZE THERE NEVER WAS

ANYTHING BUT

THOUGHT!"

Carol had been feeling low, but as Syd talked she suddenly had a glimmer of the meaning of 'no thought'. She realized her feelings of anger and jealousy were caused by thoughts. Her face changed as if by magic and she became instantly high and happy. Her face was soft and pink and Barb said Carol looked younger and more beautiful.

Tears of joy were in Carol's eyes and Syd said it was without a doubt the highest he had ever seen her. She was hearing more than anyone in the room and as Carol became high Dave went right along with her. When they left for the ferry, the transformation on their faces was amazing.

Photo by P. Minifie

CHAPTER XIV

A LOOK AT OUR CONDITIONING

Paulette, Bill's sister, and her friend Judy had come over to Salt Spring for a weekend and we took them over to Syd's. We were so excited about higher awareness that we talked about it with anyone who was interested, and Paulette and Judy wanted to meet Syd. They had also been to awareness groups and spent the afternoon asking Syd questions on his views.

He was asked if he ever became angry.

Syd replied,

"Yes, occasionally."

"But I thought you said anger was negative and one couldn't learn anything through anger?"

Syd sat gazing tranquilly out of the window for a few moments as a loaded barge made its way through the channel. He smiled and replied.

"YOUR ANGER IS UNCONTROLLED DUE TO

THE FACT THAT YOU DO NOT KNOW YOURSELF.

WHEN YOU KNOW YOURSELF

YOU KNOW THE WHOLE OF HUMANITY IS BIZARRE

WHEN YOU JOIN IN THE FUN

OF BEING BIZARRE AT THE SAME TIME

TEACH PEOPLE THE ART OF LOVE."

Judy looked puzzled,

"Are you saying anger is O.K. for you and not for me?"

Syd smiled,

"Your ego simply won't allow you to believe someone could know something that you don't. Once again, it's feeling you are too damned important. Being important is a burden, one should throw this heavy load away."

Syd sat quietly for a moment and then continued.

"Perhaps you can hear it this way. A man of knowledge has the right to be angry! The difference is that his anger is completely controlled. It is used in a positive way such as showing someone something of value as opposed to the anger you know which is negative! Beware of the tricks a man of knowledge possesses! If you ever try to figure him out, you will hear nothing but 'words'. Stop analyzing!"

Everyone in the room was smiling although Paulette and her friend appeared somewhat confused. Then Judy said,

"But you look so ordinary! You wear blue jeans and shirts and live an ordinary married life. You don't look like a Guru to me. You should want peace and tranquility and want to be more isolated."

Syd burst into laughter and as his laughter rang out, he held his chest as if in pain due to the hilarity.

"Hey, Syd, I don't see what's so funny. It makes sense to me," was the angry reply.

Once again Syd laughed and then stopped and looked very seriously at his questioner.

"Just say the word and I'll give you a guru who fills your every wish."

We all laughed and he continued,

"YOU SEE MY FRIEND

A GURU IS JUST LIKE YOU.

HE HAS THE CHOICE OF LIVING AND THINKING

ANY WAY HE WISHES.

WE ARE ALL "GURUS".

NO SELF-REALIZED PERSON

WILL DISAGREE WITH ANOTHER

REALIZED BEING.

THERE IS NOTHING TO DISAGREE ABOUT

ONLY THOSE WHO DO NOT KNOW SELF

ANALYZE AND JUDGE

ALTHOUGH THEY KNOW NOT WHAT THEY JUDGE.

JUDGING AND ANALYZING LEADS TO

BLINDNESS OF SELF!"

We later were on the subject of how males have been trying to prove their manliness for years and how many negative games are connected to upholding this image of manliness.

"A lot of our problems in this world today are caused through men trying to prove to themselves their manliness."

Bill asked Syd if this wasn't a natural way for men to feel.

"Don't you like to be called manly?"

"To me it doesn't matter. I am both male and female. Everyone on earth is both male and female but appear in this karmic life as whatever. Therefore to your question,

I AM A MAN

AND I LOVE BEING A MAN.

I LOVE BEING ME

I LOVE HOW I LOOK

I AM THE WAY I WAS CREATED

IT DOESN'T MATTER WHY I WAS CREATED AS I AM!

IT JUST IS!

"It is my illusion that I live with in this life. The beauty comes when you don't have to prove manliness! You are too busy concerning yourself with what others think of you. Society has done a good job of making you believe you must prove things. I've told you before that you must drop your past experiences and conditioning which have led you to what you are now. Try and drop competition with yourself and others. It's a heavy burden to carry and sure as hell it will pull you down to lower states of consciousness.

"To compare yourself to others is detrimental to your happiness. While you are comparing there is no chance of happiness. You are caught up in an endless game. Once you get what you think you want, you begin all over again comparing. Once again you are dissatisfied with what you have.

Our society has taught us to compete with each other in almost every facet of life. This competition creates envy, dishonesty and naturally comparison. Once you learn not to compare, you find your negative games become fewer and fewer. Then happiness and satisfaction will flow in. You will begin to see that the fruitless comparison games that people play are useless and you will have no part in them."

CHAPTER XV

THE MEANING OF GOD

Paulette and Judy were so fascinated with Syd's words that we no sooner finished breakfast the next morning when we headed back for more.

Paulette's first question was a good one.

"Syd, what would you say God is?"

"God", Syd began, "is just a word to describe the Supreme Being, yet God is everything. We hear the word God and we interpret it to suit our personal past experiences. Sometimes one's thoughts towards this word 'God' can be negative, therefore filled with disbelief. We all have our own idea of what God is but it is impossible to imagine unless you have actually realized God.

"I am sure we are aware enough that we both believe the source of happiness is inside, that is, the true Self.

"Now, I say, that the true Self, God, or whatever you want to call it are all the same thing. It is the true you. You have to start believing in yourself by taking responsibility for not only your actions, but for being here on earth. Perhaps if you start believing and taking full responsibility you will meet the true you, in God's name."

Paulette looked amazed.

"Syd, I can understand taking responsibility for my actions, but I can't take the responsibility for my being here on earth."

Syd replied,

"To take responsibility for being here on earth is what you might call a real 'Biggy'."

Smiling at our confused faces, he continued.

TO TAKE THIS RESPONSIBILITY

YOU MUST FORGET YOUR BODY

AND IMAGINE YOU ARE SELF!

TRUE SELF PICKED THE BODY

REQUIRED TO GO THROUGH LIFE

AS WE NOW KNOW LIFE.

IF YOU INSIST ON THINKING

BODY, I, ME,

YOU HAVE MISSED THE POINT ENTIRELY.

"Another way to take responsibility is to blame God for picking your body! Then if you realize you are God, once again you are responsible for picking your body!"

Bill said,

"I was once told if you have sinned, you cannot realize God!"

"Anyone who talks like this is babbling absolute rubbish. Self does not judge right from wrong nor does Self hand out sentences to keep you in a so-called place called Hell. The only hell that exists is in your own mind, put there by thought, 'your thought'. It is you who is judge and jury. It is you who can turn your life from hell to joy. The true you that is your INNER SELF, is GOD. Turn inward, find God, and then you will find joy and understanding beyond your wildest imagination."

As we talked, the tide had gone out and we decided to go down to the beach. It was overcast and raining heavily and we all bundled up and went outside. Once a year at this time seaweed would come up onto the beach and now it was piled there a foot or so deep.

It was green and reminded me of spinach, and as I walked over it my feet sunk down as if it were sponge. Mary had asked if we would gather some for her garden and we picked it up in wet green handfuls and piled it up for her. We gathered enough oysters for dinner and went home to cook them.

As always, after talking with Syd, Barb and Mary, we all felt high and came home wet and tired but contented after a fine day.

CHAPTER XVI

THE BENEFITS OF
POSITIVE THINKING

One day Bill, Gary and I had taken the ferry to Vancouver. Syd had told us that writing about our feelings was a way to get in touch with them and thus bring us closer to each other. We spent the hours on the ferry writing letters to each other.

Bill wrote,

"I was painting in the kitchen and making it beautiful for Linda and myself. I was really into it and felt the only way the job could turn out was beautifully because it was done with love.

Linda was in bed enjoying the warmth and comfort only a warm bed on a rainy morning can give and I was enjoying visiting her and loving her. It was a beautiful experience of being "HERE AND NOW". I felt so much love for Linda and knew that things would never be the same because love is what I am all about. If I don't let it flow now, it never will.

When I write to you Linda, it makes me feel good inside. I feel I am smiling from the inside and tears come to my eyes. I feel your smile go inside me, multiply and give warmth. Linda, hug me, kiss me, love me and we will all experience the beautiful results."

We wrote back and forth to each other and became incredibly high while doing so. On reading the letters over again a couple of days later we laughed and thought they sounded pretty mushy. But one afternoon when we were not feeling particularly close, we read aloud what we had written. The beautiful feelings of warmth and love we'd had while writing them returned and we were back in the space they had originated from.

* * * * * * * *

Barb and Syd had been to Mayne Island to visit Dave and Carol and told us of the wonderful time they'd had. Carol had given Syd the following letter:

"Syd has been telling us how important it is to find our true feelings, positive ones, that is! As I had been feeling pretty bogged down with my own negativity I wondered if I had any positive feelings.

For some time I have been avoiding writing to my parents to tell them what is happening in my life. This morning I wrote to them and told them I am learning to see myself and others a little more clearly and see the world as a beautiful place. The only problems we have are the ones we create ourselves. I am more peaceful and contented than ever before in my life."

When I finished the letter I felt closer to them than ever before. I had shared some of my true feelings with them. I had told them only a few very simple truths about David and myself but in the telling was the acceptance that they were true. What a wonderful feeling! The world is indeed a beautiful place and how fortunate we are to have the opportunity to learn to see it more and more beautifully all the time. By looking at 'what is' instead of 'what isn't' is a simple way of creating positive thoughts. Desire is eliminated and beautiful feelings result."

Dave and Carol visited Syd and Barb's two weeks after this experience. Carol said everything was so beautiful and easy lately.

"Things are just happening perfectly but I don't feel I am doing it. I mean I am not doing anything, it's just happening and this puzzles me."

Syd grinned from ear to ear and said,

"Beautiful, really beautiful! You have moved a great deal since our talk on 'no thought'. You should enjoy these beautiful feelings you are now having, you have earned them! To make you realize the beauty of the space you are in, I will try and explain what is happening.

"You HEARD Truth the day we spoke of 'no thought.' The wisdom which you heard led you to SEE the world from a different level. This level is much more positive, therefore you see, hear and feel more positively without trying! The simple reason being that you are NOT CREATING your negative games, 'no thought'. This is why you are high and everything is beautiful 'without trying'."

"Wow, Right! It's such a beautiful space, I just hope it lasts!"

Everyone broke into laughter and the energy in the room was once again absolutely fantastic.

CHAPTER XVII

SEEKING WISDOM

Pam and Jim were a young couple who had decided to make their home on Salt Spring Island. They had been at the first of Syd's gatherings and had not returned, but in the past couple of weeks had been coming to talk to Syd and Barb. They said they had noticed a positive change in those who had stayed and had again decided to meet with us.

Pam asked Syd,

"What are the benefits of being involved in high awareness and searching for Self?"

"AS YOU BEGIN TO TRULY SEE YOURSELF

YOU BEGIN TO SEE MORE CLEARLY!

THE MORE YOU RAISE

THIS CURTAIN OF IGNORANCE OF SELF

THE MORE INTENSE THE FEELINGS OF

LOVE AND UNDERSTANDING

BECOME.

"The world starts to slow down and everything looks and feels better and better. Then comes the stage where you become tired of looking for your Self and you simply give up searching. You will then know what you were searching for! The funny thing is, that you will realize you have known the secret all along! As a matter of fact it was so simple that you wouldn't believe it. You will laugh at it all. IN YOUR LAUGHTER WILL BE BEAUTIFUL LOVE. You will know that everything is exactly the way it should be."

Jim was wondering why it was so difficult to teach wisdom to others.

Syd stroked his beard and said,

"Wisdom cannot be explained because wisdom and mind-thinking are two separate things. When one ventures to try and explain wisdom it creates confusion to the listener. Let me try and explain it this way. The moment you realize there must be more to life than just what you see and hear, this experience is the beginning of your journey to knowledge. It is the investigation into life.

TRUE INVESTIGATION INTO

THE KNOWLEDGE OF LIFE

ALWAYS LEADS INSIDE ONE'S SELF

AND KNOWLEDGE OF ONE'S SELF

IS WISDOM.

Photo by P. Minifie

"This is why wisdom cannot be explained. It must be experienced."

"Then why do you waste your time trying to explain to people?"

"Although it cannot be explained," Syd continued, "if one tries to explain wisdom, somewhere along the line someone may hear something which triggers an encounter with wisdom."

Pam had a thoughtful look on her face and said to Syd.

"You say don't search, yet many books I have read say search and you will find."

Syd replied,

"I realize it sounds like a contradiction when I say both are true. Once again there are two levels of answers.

"You see, if you are searching, this means that you haven't yet found whatever you are searching for! Once the search ends, at that moment you realize Truth. You have stopped searching! In other words you have found what you are looking for. You stopped searching! Right now you haven't had the experience of knowing this to be true, therefore you have no other choice but to search! You see, one can search without searching. It is a matter of being truly honest with yourself and living in the here and now."

"But Syd, if you live in the here and now, how can you possibly search?"

"If you already know what your goal in life is, you don't have to keep thinking about it. Live in the here and now. It will just happen! There is no end to the search, every moment of your life will be a new experience. Every moment brings new information, the very information you are searching for. So, stop searching -- BE NOW!"

Everyone in the room was really in a high space and wanted to continue with our talks. Pam said,
"I am still confused but I feel beautiful, so I must be hearing something!"
Syd looked at her and said,
"I've told you before, don't try and figure it out, just talk and listen, it will all just come to you."
Jim asked Syd,
"What is all this fear I have of finding out who and what I am?"
"The fear you are talking about is the fear of the death of your ego."
"Wow," exclaimed Jim. "It's so damned dead-on. It blows my mind, but it is so dead-on it makes me feel beautiful."
"It is really a silly thing to fear the knowing of one-self," replied Syd. "Getting to know Self is getting to know the Kingdom of God. This Kingdom of God knows no fear!

ANYONE WHO HAS ENTERED

THE HOUSE OF GOD

KNOWS FEAR IS ONLY THOUGHT

AND IN HIS HOUSE

ALL THOUGHTS ARE POSITIVE.

THIS IS WHY GOD-SELF IS LOVE.

Around midnight we all went down to the beach. We took flashlights and gathered oysters and dug for some small butter clams. The moon was full and it was a fine, clear night. We were all having a wonderful time and later returned to the house, steamed open the clams and oysters and ate them with lemon and melted butter. I felt so close to everyone, and the house was full of laughter, warmth and love.

CHAPTER XVIII

WHAT IS MIND?

It was Friday night and we gathered together again to learn. Barb, who very rarely said much during our discussions, looked over at Syd and asked,

"What is mind?"

"The mind is non-existent to anyone who has realized Self! This so-called mind is only thought. Without thought there is no mind! When the knowledge of this fact is experienced there is direct contact with Self. When this direct contact occurs then one sees clearly. One sees Truth because there are no thoughts to analyze or judge.

"Although it appears that an Enlightened person uses his mind like everyone else, this is not so! He simply plays the game of life and acts like anyone else. The difference is he knows his acts are that of an actor so he enjoys playing his role in life, knowing that nothing matters!"

"But if nothing really matters how can you enjoy yourself?"

"This is rather difficult to explain in words, perhaps we should try and experience it.

"Have you ever sat looking at a beautiful breathtaking scene? At the moment you really FEEL the beauty, 'nothing really matters'. You became caught up in the illusion of the world, which is a beautiful experience. At the moment you realized the scene was beautiful you brought in thought and the beauty starts to disappear. Somewhere you are analyzing and judging the scene, you are comparing this scene with others in your past history! With all this comparison going on in your head how can you possibly enjoy 'what is?'

"Because a person is living here and now, 'no thought', doesn't mean to say he is an introvert! On the contrary, he will be open to anyone or anything, he will be full of love and understanding. His energy level will also be full, his so-called mind sharp and clear."

"Why is it you sometimes ask us to think about things! Then you say drop thought?"

"Of course you must think about things, you know no other way! Say for instance I ask you to think about all the things you are searching for in yourself. Then I ask you to look deep into your so-called subconscious for the answers. It's just a matter of time until you start realizing different truths about yourself.

AT THIS POINT OF REALIZING TRUTHS,

YOU CAN REST ASSURED

THAT YOU GAVE UP THINKING THOUGHTS

TO LET THE TRUTH IN.

"It's like looking at a TV set with poor reception. The poor reception is caused by too many thoughts in the atmosphere. Now if all thoughts drop away, the atmosphere clears and so does your TV reception.

NOW EVERYTIME YOU GET A CLEAR RECEPTION

THIS GIVES YOU MORE KNOWLEDGE

WHICH ALSO GIVES YOU MORE

POWER TO SEARCH

DEEPER INTO YOURSELF!"

Mary said,
"Sometimes when I am talking to someone I feel guilty and frustrated that I am not really hearing what is going on. I start to condemn what I hear."
Syd replied,
"If you listen to someone talking and disagree with what he is saying be careful not to condemn without first looking into yourself. You may not be hearing what the other party is saying because your own hang-ups are not allowing you to listen properly. It is too big a threat to your 'ego'. You judge to suit yourself, hearing nothing but your own thoughts. One should be very careful in such a situation. It's a contracted outlook on life with no chance of finding yourself. One should truly look at oneself to expand.

BE ADVENTUROUS

AND TREAD THE PATH

TO THE SECRET OF HEAVEN.

THIS IS ACCOMPLISHED

BY BEING OPEN AND HONEST

WITH YOURSELF

START TO SEE THINGS AS THEY ARE

NOT WHAT YOU WANT THEM TO BE.

CHAPTER XIX

THE TRUE SPIRIT OF CHRISTMAS

It is now Christmas. We are together with Barb and Syd and the family. The room is beautiful with the warm glow of the fire, cedar boughs over the mantle, holly, and a lovely Christmas tree in the comer. Everyone is joyous with the warmth of the Christmas spirit.

Syd's daughter Susan said,

"Imagine, Christmas will soon be over again."

Syd burst into laughter, put his hand on top of her head and said,

"Don't give Christmas up, after all, it's only a FEELING of love and understanding. You are the one who creates this FEELING, so why not keep it going and every day will be Christmas!"

Susan looked a bit surprised and said,

"I can't possibly afford to do that!"

Syd roared once again and said,

"You can't afford not to! It isn't the giving or receiving of presents that is important. It is the giving of love and understanding that matters.

HE WHO GIVES LOVE

WILL SURELY

RECEIVE LOVE!

LOVE FLOWS FROM A VESSEL

WHICH CANNOT BE

EMPTIED!

AS YOU GIVE

MORE AND MORE LOVE

THE VESSEL OVERFLOWS!

CHAPTER XX

THE VALUE OF LISTENING TO AN
ENLIGHTENED MAN

We all knew the book was nearing an end and one evening Syd turned to me and said,

"I hope your book will be a success. Not for fame and fortune but with the hope that someone else may obtain from your words the wisdom which you and Bill received by writing them.

"I have in a very short space of time seen both of you change before my eyes. You came as blind mixed-up people with no idea what relationship you had to the rest of the world, nor what purpose you had in life. You were floundering like fish out of water. Now my eyes behold two beautiful people who have stopped floundering and have found the needed wisdom to guide to greater things.

"With this new found wisdom I see you as lovers, loving as you have never loved before. This new-found love comes with wisdom. It is wisdom!

"Perhaps someday we may together write another book and share the language of love and understanding to describe wisdom, so that others may benefit."

* * * * * * * *

When I first began to work on this book, awareness was uppermost in my mind. The growth of the book has convinced me of my own personal growth. Many new experiences and feelings are slowly changing the day-to-day pattern of life in a positive way. A time has come when the feeling of love in our home is so overpowering as to offer concrete proof of the values of listening to an enlightened man.

Bill and Gary, Barb and Syd, our friends, our home, the book, all have become an increasing source of joy and happiness. Outside influences are less important. The whole trip is such a fine and real thing to be doing. Home has a meaning it has never had before. I think less and less of myself and more of others, of Gary and Bill, and as this happens, I love them in a new and better way. I also feel more love being returned. The story has changed to a love story.

Syd's love and knowledge has enriched the lives of all those who listen. His love is like an unwavering beacon to guide and help us all.

We are all in the same room, in the same space, talking about love and where and how we find it. Syd is looking at us and saying,

IT IS IMPOSSIBLE TO SPREAD

THE BLANKET OF LOVE

OVER EVERYONE IN THE UNIVERSE.

IT IS TOO BIG AND HEAVY A BLANKET.

GATHER UP ALL YOUR FORCES

AND RETREAT INWARDLY

FROM THERE YOU WILL SEE

EVERYTHING IS LOVE

YOU HAVE FOUND THE MAGIC BLANKET

END

CPSIA information can be obtained at www.ICGtesting.com
Printed in the USA
LVOW10s1817211015

459187LV00001B/13/P